"Wendy Rainey's streetwise world-watching writings inspired by the gritty realities of her tough-love time and place in her generation's modern day hard-knocked life combined with her unique warmth, uncompromising compassion and wisdom enlightens and amazes her reader time and time again with her wordsmithery and extraordinary and oft-times heartbreaking—but always caregiving—veracity."

Joan Jobe Smith, author of *Tales of an Ancient Go-go Girl*

"Ever since I first read the work of Wendy Rainey I've been blown away, it's like we were siblings trapped on the same school bus--in the same little moment of time. It sounds almost cliché to talk about how quickly time goes by after a certain age, but inside all of us, there is that scared kid waiting for the bus, waiting the future that may never come or turn out the way we hope it will. Wendy is still that girl on the highway and her own history is her battlefield, but her words prove time and time again, that we're all in this together."

John Dorsey, author of *Your Daughter's Country*

"Picture a girl with scars that don't show. She's on a highway hitchhiking. She's wearing a USC varsity sweater she got cheap at a thrift shop. She's carrying a battered suitcase, not much inside. The girl has seen every kinda thing but she's not broken. She will give you a chance, but don't cross her. This is the protagonist I pictured when I read Wendy Rainey's extraordinary new chapbook, Girl On The Highway. The poems will break your heart, then educate and inspire you. She will enchant you, too. Buy this book."

Suzanne O'Connell, author of *What Luck*

GIRL ON THE HIGHWAY

WENDY RAINEY

GIRL ON THE HIGHWAY

pictureshowpress.net

Cover by Curtis Hayes

FIRST EDITION

ISBN-13: 978-1-7324144-8-8
ISBN-10: 1-7324144-8-3

I am grateful to the following people for their support and their talent: Curtis Hayes, Kevin Ridgeway, Suzanne O'Connell, Joan Jobe Smith, Hiram Sims, John Dorsey, Jack Grapes, Catfish McDaris, Carol Anne Perini, and Penelope Lowder.

Thank you to my editor and publisher, Shannon Phillips, for her sharp eye and her dedication.

A special shout-out to Gatsby Books in Long Beach, CA.

CONTENTS

Sweaters of the Dead

When I was young,
I wore the clothes of dead people
I bought at the Salvation Army.
The sweaters of the dead
kept me warm
as I rode my bicycle through Hollywood
and waited for the bus on 4th and Grand.

One of my favorite sweaters
had a label sewn into the neck:
A Mrs. Blanche Culpepper Original
Knitted for Mimi.
I found the beaded cashmere cardigan
in a bargain bin for $3.00.
Mrs. Blanche Culpepper,
I picture you waving to me
in a field of sunflowers
whose heads are swaying in the wind.
Their green stems are winding their way
up Fairfax Avenue.
I was lost, Blanche,
always waiting for the bus before dawn,
but kept warm in the sunflower sweater
you knitted for Mimi.

And Bobby Alvarez,
who gave your 1948 USC Varsity sweater
to the women's auxiliary in Van Nuys?
It should have been kept in a cedar chest
filled with moth balls.
Instead I wore it to the bar every weekend.
Soaked in sweat,
and sloshed in beer.
I never got the blood stain out of the left sleeve
from the belt fight two punks had one night.

I got so drunk once
that I fell face down in the street
and got a taste of the gutter.
Sort of like the dirt you tasted
when you slid into home base
that one last time.

I remember the sad sweaters that found me,
sweaters desperate for love
and attention;
the plaid mohair
with a disintegrated condom
in an inner concealed pocket.
And the bowling sweater
belonging to Darla Baranowski
from the Tarzana Bowling League.
Her name was emblazoned in sequins across the chest.
On the back were two bowling balls
with an erect pin between them.
I wore it proudly.

There were the angora sweater sets
so soft to the touch
that strangers on the street would stroke them
without my consent.
I named them after movie stars;
Natalie Wood,
Marilyn Monroe,
Lana Turner,
and the sweater with the floating pineapples
was my Carmen Miranda.

When I was young,
I rode the buses,
walked the streets,
and worked the jobs
in the sweaters of the dead.

The sweaters kept me warm.
The sweaters told me their secrets.
The sweaters listened to mine.
I see them on a circular rack in a junk shop
off of Magnolia in Burbank.
The sweaters are whispering to me.
The sweaters are reaching for me.
The sweaters are beckoning me
back home
to that bus stop on Wilshire and Fairfax
where I will always be standing alone
in the dark,
waiting for the dawn to come.

Where did you go, Joyce Finkelstein?

I dreamed of you last night, Joyce.
You were standing on the grass
in your paisley shirt,
between the jungle gym
and the Jacaranda tree.
Some boys were playing catch with your beret.
Laughing and screaming,
the two Brendas shoved you back and forth,
until you fell to the ground.
You got up,
but they knocked you down again,
so you got on your back,
and kicked at them
with your suede shoes.
I ran over to help you,
but you were spinning on your back by then,
kicking at Tammy and Kimberly,
who were now turning away from you
and descending on me.
Their pigtails whipped through the air
as they pushed me to the grass.
I stood up,
balled my fist,
and smashed it into their flowered dresses.

Sometimes I think of you, Joyce,
when I'm trying to get home on the 405.
You sat at the desk next to mine.
You wore a plastic patch over your left eye
that clipped onto your glasses.
You had a slight lisp,
and on occasion you stuttered,
but when you spoke,
kids turned around in their chairs and listened.
Mr. Wadinski stapled the John Lennon poster

you brought to class
on the board near our desks.
The word IMAGINE floated above your head.

I can't remember the day you moved away,
but I remember sitting on the shag carpet
in your parent's living room,
watching The World at War.
Your father came in with his tumbler of Cutty Sark
and changed the channel.
He didn't want us to see the footage
of the prisoners of war,
or the explosions,
or the piles of dead bodies.
After he left to get more booze,
you got up and changed the channel
back to The World at War.
Stretching out onto the carpet, you smiled,
slipped off your shoes,
reached into the pretzel bag:
"They never want me to know what's really going on,
but I always find out anyway."

What I Know About My Stepfather

When I was ten
I found his scuba gear,
his hang glider,
and his saxophone,
in the garage.
"Why don't you do any of these fun things
anymore, dad?"
Without skipping a beat
he told me that after he took on
four kids,
a wife,
a dog,
two cats,
and a mortgage,
that was about as much fucking fun
as he could handle.

Spaghetti and Milk

When you said
you wanted to get in the car
and drive as far away from us as possible,
and never see us again,
I didn't believe you.

When you said you were sick of every last one of us,
and you wished abortion had been legal,
and that it would have solved all of your problems,
I thought it was the wine talking.

I remember your disgust
as you flung the plate of spaghetti into the air.
Worms and blood rained all over me.
The bottle you chucked over my head
smashed against the kitchen wall.
Streams of milk
trickled down the wallpaper
and onto the kitchen floor,
where the kitten lapped at my feet.

When you told me to clean up the mess
I walked over to the ashtray beside you,
took a drag off your Pall Mall,
and blew smoke into your face.
I was thirteen.
What did I know about the human condition?

But I forgive you now,
not because I think you didn't mean it,
but because I know that you did.

The Ice Cream Cone

My Grandmother liked her Harvey Wallbangers.
She had a few too many one afternoon.
It wasn't unusual and I didn't think much of it
until she leaned in and slurred,
"Your mother had a nickname for her father's penis."
She lit a cigarette and took a drag.
She called it "The Ice Cream Cone."
She threw her head back and laughed.
I could see her gold filings
and smell the vodka on her breath.
She blew a smoke ring toward me
and poked her finger through it.
Perspiration broke out on my upper lip.
"Funny thing. Your mom went through a period
where she kept flushing her underpants down the toilet."
She giggled.
The clam chowder I had for lunch was coming back up.
I swirled it around in my mouth.
"You feeling OK? You don't look so good."
She dipped a tortilla chip into a bowl of guacamole,
crunching and redipping.
"Be a dear and make me a fresh cocktail."
She held out her glass.
I grabbed her tumbler,
went into the kitchen and smashed it in the sink,
cutting my hand on the shards.
Blood dripped onto her white shag carpet
as I walked back into the living room toward her.
"You let Grandpa babysit mom."
"Oh, yes," she smiled,
extinguishing her cigarette in the crystal ashtray.
"She was always his favorite."
"You let grandpa babysit me."
 She reached toward me.
"Where's my drink, Hon?"

She looked at the red stain on my dress
and sat up in her easy chair.
Her mouth fell open as she watched my hand drip blood
onto her custom made white suede sofa.
"What the hell have you done?" she screamed at me,
looking around the room.
"Where did all this blood come from?"

The Acrobat

They came for my brother on a Sunday afternoon
in the middle of a heat wave.
They came for him
after he had shattered all seventeen windows
in the house
with a baseball bat.

Wearing only a red Speedo,
he climbed to the top of our Sycamore tree,
and hung upside down from a branch,
waving to the crowd in our yard.

Our neighbors turned their heads
toward the sound of the siren,
drowning out the melody
of the ice cream truck,
as the ambulance pulled into our driveway.
And out they jumped,
two husky men in white coats.
The one holding a clipboard
commanded my brother to come down from the tree.

My brother sprang from the Sycamore to the lawn,
somersaulting through the sprinklers,
rolling and tumbling away from the muddied orderlies
who had collided with each other on the lawn.

The neighbors lined the sidewalk in front of our house,
lapping their ice cream bars,
as my brother leapt over the fallen men.
Trailing away in a flourish of backflips,
he turned to the crowd and took a bow.

He scaled the fence to our backyard,
climbed the ladder to the high dive,

and executed a reverse dive
with a half twist in the pike position,
and began swimming the butterfly.

The orderlies sat on lawn chairs
at the edge of the pool,
cheering my brother as he swam laps.
One of them pulled a cigarette from his pocket,
lit it, flicking ashes into the pool.

In my dream,
my brother is not strapped to a gurney
or taken to a mental hospital.
He never becomes a shut-in
or the town freak,
nor does he sit in a La-Z-Boy recliner
and watch game shows for twelve hours at a stretch.

In my dream,
my brother is jumping on his trampoline
in our backyard.
The sun shines on his face and hair.
He laughs as he bounces higher and higher into the sky.
Anything seems possible.

And then I hear the shattering of glass
like a baseball bat smashing windows.
I see my brother soaring through a crack in the atmosphere.
My brother the acrobat
tumbles into infinity.

That Great Big Beautiful Bastard

My father died alone on a Christmas Day
in ninety degree heat on a bus bench in Las Vegas.
His death certificate read cirrhosis of the liver.
I wasn't surprised.
He had been handsome
and even after he married my mother,
he had so many girlfriends
that in high school I joked
that I was afraid I would accidentally date my own kin.
The day my youngest brother was born, he disappeared
only to resurface two weeks later
with a wad of cash for my mom.
He threw it on the dining room table,
claiming he had another family to support,
living sixteen miles from us.

It isn't for me to know why or how
my father's head was split open
outside the Honey Bucket Saloon in Reno,
or what he thought about during the fourteen years
he served out a manslaughter conviction
in Nevada State Prison.
It isn't for me to know why he thought it was a good idea
to call me from Nova Scotia on my ninth birthday
when he had promised to be at my party in Long Beach.
He was ecstatic, telling me about the Northern Lights,
and how he would take me to see them someday.
When my mother grabbed the phone from me,
she hissed under her breath, "Go to hell, you prick."

I don't know my father,
but I remember the look on his face
as I jumped off of the kitchen table one morning.
With one hand he scooped me off the linoleum
and held me to his chest.

He stroked my hair as I screamed.
He kissed my nose
and set me down into the sink
to let the cold water wash the blood off my knees,
and the tears off my face.

My father died alone on a Christmas day.
The sun was blazing in the December sky.
My father keeled over on a bus bench
and fell to the pavement,
leaving only an empty fifth of Four Roses Whiskey behind.

My father;
that drunk,
that murderer,
that wife beater,
that burned-out womanizing scum.

That great big beautiful bastard.

Girl On The Highway

I saw her wandering along the side of Highway 89A
on a fifteen-mile stretch of Arizona road
between Cottonwood and Sedona.
The embers she flicked from her cigarette
sparked in the dark.
She was wearing cowboy boots, a cropped top,
and cut-off jeans.
She looked about eighteen.
Her brown hair hung past her waist,
covering her frayed shorts.
As I passed, I recognized her as a waitress
who had recently been fired from Bob's Café,
a restaurant where I worked most weekends.
I stopped my car and called out the window,
"What're you doing out here, Sherry?
Car break down?"
She threw her cigarette butt onto the highway,
walked over to the passenger side,
stuck her head through the open window.
"No," she said, staring at me.
Her face glowed with perspiration.
I reached over and opened the door.
She settled into the seat,
propping her cowboy boots onto the dashboard.
I watched her run her black fingernails through her hair,
twisting it into an enormous bun on top of her head,
securing it with two Bic Pens
she had found in a 7-11 cup.
The head of a boa constrictor
appeared at the nape of her neck
and was apparently wrapping itself
around her entire body.
I saw it's tail disappear into her boots.
 "Where do you live?"
"Cottonwood," she rolled her eyes, smirking.

I pulled out onto the highway and made a U-turn,
driving my car back to Cottonwood.
She looked out the window, snapping her gum
and blowing bubbles.
I offered her a bottle of water
from the grocery bag in the back seat.
She grabbed it,
downing it in under a minute.
"Sorry, A.C. doesn't work," I said.
She pressed her gum onto the windshield,
took an apple out of the Ralph's bag and ate it,
throwing the core out the window.
I offered her some Chips Ahoy.
She snatched the box,
stuffed the cookies into her mouth,
and washed them down with a pint of milk she found
at the bottom of the grocery bag.
When she was finished,
she took a pack of gum from her pocket,
unwrapped it,
and shoved it all into her mouth,
throwing the gum wrappers onto the car floor.
"It isn't safe out here at night, Sherry."
"No shit, Einstein." She popped a bubble in my face
and turned her head away from me.
She gave Bob's Café the finger as we rolled into Cottonwood.
I asked her what street she lived on.
"Just drop me off at the Dragonfly."
I pulled into the parking lot of the Dragonfly Saloon.
We drove by a couple of bikers smoking near a dumpster.
The bald one smiled, flashing his gold incisors.
His friend made a V with his fingers,
flicking his tongue like a lizard.
Megadeth pulsated through the bar walls.
"Sherry, you don't have to do this.
Do you have parents anywhere?"
She looked me in the eye for the first time.

"You some kinda lesbo?" she giggled.
"The cooks all think you're a lesbo."
I looked at her chubby face
in the harsh light of the street lamp.
Reaching across her lap, I opened the car door.
She strutted across the parking lot
past the motorcycles and beaten-up pickups,
past the drunks stumbling to their vehicles.
A grey haired biker opened the bar door for her.
She threw her hands up and broke into gyrations.
I could hear her laughing
as the men cheered inside.
But all I could see was a boa constrictor
disappearing into her cowboy boots
as the door swung shut behind her.

Girlie Show

It's the spotlight glaring in my eyes
that saves me the sight of anyone's face.
While striding the stage I tear off my dress
and it flies up behind me like a pair of wings.
I imagine I'm strutting the roof of a high-rise
and when I look down,
I see the rats and roaches crawling the surface of the earth,
I look up and I am blinded by the sun.

But I must tread the edge of the skyscraper in stiletto heels,
naked,
my wings spread behind me,
the music blaring,
lifting me above the laughter of the hyenas
as they feed, and drink,
and watch.

Hollywood Success

There was nothing to suggest greatness
unless you counted the vastness of the Arizona desert
which doubled as a movie set.
The horse she rode in on was an anguished creature,
caught and trapped in a faraway land
and brought back to Burbank to be whipped and broken
and led away in chains.
If you look into that beast's eyes
you will know what it is to be terrified,
not of anything in particular,
but the sheer monotony of the carnival carousel,
the sea of eyes
and the horrible laughter of the popcorn munchers,
the screamers,
the peeing and sweating mob—
the way they feed on the meat of the beast.
They want the beast to be funnier,
they want the beast to be bloodier,
they want the beast to kill or be killed,
they want to eat the flesh of the beast and become the beast
but they cannot,
these multitudes who demand so much from the beast
but give nothing in return.
And she, the girl with knees that bend
in front of powerful men
and a head that bops like a turkey on their members.
She who rides the beast with a gloved hand and an orchid between
her legs
that spread onscreen.
She with a body into which they all want to dip their fingers
and taste and eat
and rip open with the juices running down their chins.
And you,
who work in offices, you who are teachers, lawyers,
mechanics,

and dentists,
you mothers with a baby at your breast,
you who left your wife for someone else's,
you who left Nebraska because you were bored—
when you go to that dark temple to pray
look up into her eyes
and you will see a vacancy there
that we have mistaken for greatness—
as vast as the Arizona desert.

The Streetwise Barbarian

This is for the pit bull who clamped his jaws
around my dog's throat
as we walked down my street on a sunny Tuesday afternoon.
And for the junkie from the halfway house who startled me
by wielding a screwdriver in my face
as I emptied the trash in my pajamas.
And the dude at Vons who crashed his cart into mine,
chatted me up, then appeared from behind
as I loaded my trunk with groceries.
Yes, come follow me out to my car in the underground parking lot.
I have something I want to show you in the back seat.
Let's party, just you, me, and my new toy.
I'll do crazy ass things to your body you'll never forget.
I'll make you scream like a bitch in heat.
My new toy has 65 million volts of FUCK YOU.
After I shock you three or four times,
you'll lose all control of your bowels,
shitting your pants,
at which point I'll take the spiked end of my new toy
and spend the next five minutes tenderizing your meat.
When you come to, I will shine the strobe in your eyes and push
the little red button that delivers an
earsplitting siren.
After several rounds of that you'll collapse
onto the concrete, begging for your mommy.
And I'll do it all with one hand
because I'll need the other one free
to livestream it on my smartphone, of course.

Melania

We want to feel sorry for you
because your husband cheats on you
with strippers
and Russian prostitutes.
We suspect that your son has a disability,
and that you are abused, terrified,
and being held captive by a fascist dictator.
Give us a signal—
something bolder
than the usual recoiling of your hand from his,
and we'll send in the Marines
or Tom Cruise.

Melania,
we want to get comedians fired
and ruined for life
to save you and your son
from ever being the butt
of anybody's joke again.
We saw by the way you eschewed heavy makeup
and expensive clothes
at the toddler internment camp
that you were deeply effected
by the Honduran children screaming for their mothers.

Oh, Melania,
you are a woman we are told, who speaks five languages,
a woman with impeccable fashion sense.
We know you didn't mean it
when your $39.00 jacket declared,
"I really don't care. Do you?"

Melania, we want to lay down our bodies
in the mud
so that you may walk all over us

in your Louboutin heels.
Maybe you can spear
some of those caged babies
with your stilettos
and kick them
—humanely—
back to the hell they came from.
Melania,
take our social security,
our health care,
the after school music program,
and the food stamps from gramma's cookie jar,
and buy yourself a dozen gold plated G-strings.

Melania,
please know,
we never intentionally ogled your nude breasts
and waxed pudendum on the internet,
but those free-spirited photos just keep popping up.
We can't be expected to look away,
can we?

The Feral Children of Los Angeles

A pack of feral children was spotted walking northbound
alongside the 101/Hollywood Freeway in Cahuenga Pass
just after 6:00 a.m.
during the Monday morning commute.
The leader of the pack
appears to be a ten year-old girl
traveling with three other children,
ages five, seven, and eight.
The four were seen engaged in a feeding frenzy
just off the Barnham exit
where a big rig operator was sighted
throwing a bag of Big Macs onto the highway.
At 1 p.m. on Tuesday, the pack was spotted
outside an oceanfront bistro.
Patrons of the restaurant were traumatized
as the emaciated children foraged in the dumpster,
stuffing their mouths with cider-brined pork chops
and braised beef belly.
Maple bacon chutney sauce
with wild blackberry liqueur
dripped down their chins
and onto their naked bodies
as they danced and howled,
smearing black cod brûlée
on their faces and rubbing it in their hair.

Counselors were on hand
for a group of Malibu wives.
One wife stated,
"So, we were walking to our cars after brunch
and we see these filthy children gorging on garbage.
I was like, this is some totally edgy shit!
I gotta document this scene for my blog.
But those little savages
wouldn't even stand still for a fuckin' photo."

Animal researchers have noticed
an increase in pack sightings
over the past few weeks.
"We have known for years
about the feral children of Los Angeles.
We don't know how many of them there are.
Up until now they have secluded themselves
in the Hollywood Hills
and surrounding Santa Monica Mountains.
This recent rash of sightings
may have been necessitated by drought conditions.
Some of our research suggests
that the children have been raised by coyotes
which accounts for the child-like howling
that residents have reported hearing at night."

Experts caution that the youths have developed a taste
for four-star cuisine.
"But if these children are unable to scavenge the kind of food
they have grown accustomed to
then anyone who routinely dines in restaurants
rated with more than two Michelin Stars
is at risk for an attack.
"Those who engage in rigorous physical activity
tend to develop muscle and sinew throughout the body
that make their meat tougher," the coroner explained,
"Hence, they are in the low risk group.
A daily workout alone
will not guarantee one's safety," he warned.
"These youngsters have, in a very short time,
cultivated a highly sophisticated palate.
They are on the hunt for soft flesh
that has been marinated in expensive port
and gourmet cuisine."

Bloggers at Winelyfe.com speculate
that when the children taste the flesh of their prey,

they are tasting "Hints of Demerol and Vicodin,
lifted by kale juice and coconut water,
steeped in a deep bitter brooding,
characterized by self-indulgence
flirting with regret
and the inability to age gracefully."

Authorities are still investigating
the attack that occurred Wednesday night
as two Pacific Palisades residents
dined on their terrace.
All that was found at the scene
were their leather yoga pants
and a pair of six inch Gucci stilettos.
Their bodies have yet to be recovered.

Dinner at Denny's

I worked ten hour shifts, six days a week, for a solid year at the Denny's in Burbank. I breathed, ate, and lived Denny's. I became a monster, a monster in a yellow polyester apron. During that year I entered into one of the darkest periods of my life. Every day seemed to bring new insight into the depths of degradation that the human race was capable of sinking to. I started to notice the gluttonous tendencies of the general public. I witnessed their insatiable hunger for butter, fat, lard, gravy, syrup, and sugar. Most people enjoyed their lettuce salad drenched in a mayonnaise dressing, but there was usually more dressing than actual greens on the plate. I noticed the irritated way in which they demanded more potatoes, more beef, more sausage, and more bacon. A lot of people talked with their mouths full, spitting and spewing their food while giving me orders. Their mouths were covered with spaghetti sauce or shiny oil from the fat of the meat they ate. Their teeth were yellow from tartar and tobacco. Their breath was bad from indigestion. They farted into their underpants and belched into their napkins, and in some cases right into my face. I could see it and smell it all. Sometimes after people ate, they would loosen their belts or undo the top button of their pants and try to push the table away from them to allow more room for their bellies to expand, but the tables at Denny's were bolted down. They would stand up and lift the heavy chairs to a more comfortable distance then sit back down, looking as if they had just run a marathon. It was the greed for more and more food. Not nutritious, life sustaining, life celebrating food, but junk food to fill the void in their junky lives. And speed was key. They didn't seem to understand the concept that most of the food they ordered actually had to be cooked before it was served. And this could take some time. I could tell by looking at their complexions that they were used to existing on pre-cooked fast foods. They were used to the quick drive through combo: burger, fries, and a coke on the way back to the office, followed by irritation, constipation, and flatulence. There they were, chomping on McNuggets on the bumper-to-bumper drive home, cussing and spilling their dipping sauce on the car seat. Once safe in their living rooms, the quick phone call to Domino's Pizza, or better yet, a microwavable, frozen pizza, ready in minutes. There's a nervousness to people hooked on junk food. There's an emptiness to the eyes. So short tempered and impatient were these kinds of people that often they would gather their family and get up and walk out the door rather than wait another five minutes for their meal to be prepared. But before they'd leave the restaurant , there would be a quick stop at the register to place a complaint about their waitress for being "too slow" or having an "attitude problem."

As time went on, the different people I waited on started to assume the faces and bodies of animals and beasts. Sometimes I would imagine a combination baboon dog-boy or the face of a swine on the body of a woman, or a group of slothful children inhabiting the bodies of a pack of pit bulls. A group of young girls came in and ordered ice cream sundaes. They each got their makeup mirrors out and started to apply lipstick, eyeliner, and foundation. As I looked at them more closely, I noticed that they were gradually transforming themselves into orangutans. And soon, the vanity of their primping gave way to their prehensile hands picking lice out of each other's hair. The confidence and pride they had had in their appearance, that knowing look in the eyes of popular girls, was replaced by the look of a more trusting innocence of their simian ancestors. A couple in their thirties came in at the height of the dinner rush hour. I looked at their booth in the corner of the restaurant and cast my eyes under their table. The woman's black panties were around her ankles. The man sitting next to her had his hand in her lap. Over his hand the woman had piled a bunch of paper napkins. I could see his hand in her crotch, steadily working away. They were both staring straight ahead at nothing. It was then that I imagined the whole room, a crowd of pig-faced, monkey-eyed people, some human, some half-beast, some old, some young, all stripping. They all started to take each other's clothing off. Then the copulating began, on the floors, on the tables, in the aisles, in the vinyl booths, and up against the walls. Some used the leather chairs to bend over their partners, some straddled each other on the floor. Old men sniffed out young girls, took them from behind, pumping their buttocks, and screaming. Old women were on all fours being fucked by their husbands. The girls who had turned into orangutans were racing around the room, throwing their own feces at one another. Some were in group arrangements where oral was being performed on one person by several different animals of both sexes. There were sandwiches of people and beasts, threesomes screaming, and groaning, and grinding. They were all making the most ungodly noises. The whole restaurant was full of naked people and animals, fucking and sucking, and grunting. On the bread counter a donkey man had his face buried between a woman's legs. He flipped her over, pulled her ass cheeks apart, and dove his head in. Just then, I felt something wet hit my arm. It was a towel. The manager had thrown it at me. He liked to throw things. "Get these tables cleaned up, girlie," he said, "This place is starting to look like the inside of a zoo cage!"

The Children Are Coming For Us

after e.e. cummings

We thought we were being so careful with the children,
driving them everywhere
instead of making them walk.
Listening to the evening news
you would have thought there was a child abduction
every five minutes.
I joked that I wanted to roll them in bubble wrap
and hide them from the bogeyman.
Instead I dressed them in yoga pants
while they learned to walk,
scheduled classes and playdates
before they were out of diapers,
activated the V-chip before they could talk.
When I was caught in the sandbox
saying No to the children
a group of moms went online,
calling me a squelcher of ego,
a murderer of dreams.
I devoured every child-rearing book
I could get my hands on.
Each new bestseller,
each new school of thought
contradicted the previous trend.
Baby sign language, Baby Einstein, Bringing Up Bébé.
And the kale wraps,
the edamame shakes,
the gluten free organic soy chips,
while on the sly
I was the nanny
with a Big Mac on her breath.

And now, when I drive by an elementary school
and see a line of SUVs wrapped around the block,

collecting and depositing their precious cargo,
I want to scream,
Set them free!
Let the children ride their bikes alone
down the middle of the street
and feel, as we did,
the wind whipping through their hair.
Let the rain fall on their faces and soak their clothes.
Let them trip into this puddle-wonderful world
and roll in its mud lusciousness.
They'll scrape their knees on the cement,
but don't run for a Band-Aid right away.
Let the children bleed just enough
to learn what pain can teach them.

Strawberry, I wasn't lying
when I told you that you are a unique and precious flower.
Londyn and Kingdym, it's good to be different.
But what I should have also told you
is that you are only one minnow
swimming among billions of minnows
in a sea of diminishing returns.
Your ordinariness
is probably the most profound
and lovable thing about you.

But lately when I catch wind of the latest internet pile-on,
it is your faces that appear in my dreams.
Seeking warmth in the glow of the computer screen,
you are hunched over your keyboards
like seniors at bingo night.
Pajamaed warriors of justice,
sensitivity readers
with your butt hurt
and your porn
and your anxiety disorders.

Before you come for me, kids,
before the big call-out
and the doxxing,
let's go outside into the fresh air and sunshine
one last time.
I'll set you free
in a puddle-luscious field
where it is always Spring.
You will always be young
and dancing with marbles
and running from piracies,
while the little lame bogeyman whistles
far
and
wee.

Glorious Morning

The neon tits were flashing
at Vinnie's adult bookstore
across from my bustop
on Victory and Van Nuys.
The smell of urine and exhaust hung in the air.
I stood in the dark at 4:58 a.m.,
a can of pepper spray in my pocket,
watching for the number 5 bus to Glendale.
Bathed in the light of the porn shop,
I noticed a bald man in a vinyl suit
with exposed ass cheeks walk out the door,
whistling "Hello Dolly."
A car honked and cat-called
as he bounced down the sidewalk,
disappearing into the darkness.
A man in a baseball cap waved
from across the street,
then jogged toward me.
"Hey, babe. How'ya doin?"
He looked me up and down,
chewing his gum.
I smelled vodka on his breath.
"My van's parked over there, so..."
He motioned to the parking lot.
I held up the can of pepper spray.
"Beat it, creep."
He followed me as I walked away
from the bus stop into the street.
"Well, you don't have to be a little cunt about it."
He spit his gum at my feet.
A car swerved around us,
honking and cursing.
As he reached for my arm
I let him have it in the face.
Screaming, he covered his eyes with his hands,
falling to his knees

in the middle of Victory Boulevard.
I sprayed him again
until the can was empty.
"Fuckin' whore.
Fuckin' twat."
The headlights of the bus were approaching.
"Next time I see you
I'm gonna fuck up your face.
I'm gonna break your..."
I swung my backpack
and hit him on the head.
He collapsed onto the asphalt with a gasp
but was able to grab hold of my ankle.
I fell in the street beside him,
kicking him with my other foot.
He let go of my ankle
as the bus approached the stop.

I ran up the steps of the bus
and put my fare into the machine.
Sweat had broken out all over my body.
"You alright, miss?" the driver asked.
"Yeah, I had to spray that guy."
"You want me to call the police?"
"No. I just need to get my paycheck.
I gotta get my car out of the shop today."

It took an hour to roll into Glendale.
I spotted Venus and Saturn in the sky.
The Big Dipper was to the north.
When I reached my stop,
the bus driver told me to take care of myself.
I turned around on the sidewalk
to wave to him,
my heart still pounding in my chest.
The sun was rising in the distance
like a giant flaming ball.
Another glorious morning, after all.

Rachel Maddow looks tired tonight

Watching the news just now,
it strikes me that Rachel Maddow has dark circles
under her eyes.
Perhaps she's worn down
by the daily onslaught of chaos
perpetuated by the leader of the free world.
I wonder if she's thinking about walking her dog
in the woods,
the chilly morning air stinging her nostrils,
his heart racing as he chases a squirrel up a pine tree.
While we speculate in our pajamas,
waiting to hear a recording of a journalist
being dismembered alive,
Schubert streams in EarPods,
drowning out the screams.
And the grinding of the bone cutter
makes his mark
on all of us.

She talks to me all day long

My brother tells me that there is a beautiful girl
who talks to him all day long.
He says her name is Lisa.
He hears her voice while he sits in his living room,
watching television and smoking.
Lisa tells him to get in his car
and drive to a seafood restaurant in San Pedro Harbor.
Once there, he gets jittery in the lobby waiting to be seated.
"Pretend to talk on your cell phone
so people think you're normal."
He pulls his cell from his pocket
and begins talking to her directly.
"I don't know how to act today, Lisa," he says.
"Things are closing in on me."
"Ask the waitress about her arthritic cat."
He is given a seat with a view of the harbor.
She tells him to order the steamed oysters.
He forces a smile at a young woman
who puts a basket of sour dough and butter in front of him.
He can feel that she knows he has always lived alone.
He picks up his cell phone again.
"Lisa, are you there?"
"Look out the window," she says, "I'm watching you."
He looks.
Sea gulls fly in the distance.
A lone seal breaks the surface of the water and disappears.
He sees Lisa standing on a sail boat wearing a bikini.
She is waving to him, the cell phone to her ear.
"Now leave a generous tip and smile
so people don't think you're crazy."
Lisa drops the cell phone into the ocean,
takes off her sunglasses,
and dives into the water.
His hands shake as he pulls a comb from his shirt pocket,
checking his hair reflected in the glass.
He watches her cut across the water,
swimming closer and closer toward him.

The Sleeping Deer

Dan is ninety-three,
blind,
hard of hearing,
and unable to walk on his own.
Three times a week
I go to his house to care for him
while his wife runs errands.
I help him do his exercises,
give him his medications,
prepare his food,
and listen to his stories.

He worked the beat in Hollenbeck
in the '50's and '60's.
"I had the misfortune of being partnered
with a perv for awhile."
Dan told me that his partner
enjoyed making women undress
during routine traffic stops at night.
"I had to figure out how to get rid of him."
"How did you do it, Dan?"
 "I'm not telling you.
But I will say he never bothered anyone again."
He smiled as he took a bite of his cookie
and sipped his coffee.
"A little street justice, Dan?"
He stared straight ahead still smiling.

Almost everyone Dan knows is either dead
or dying.
He received a call a few weeks ago,
informing him that his best friend
had died in his sleep.
He was ninety-six.
"Jesus Christ, they're dropping like flies,"

he laughed,
taking a sip from a tumbler of scotch.
"When's it gonna be my turn?" he asked,
still laughing.

Last Tuesday Dan told me to get his .38 Special
from under the kitchen sink.
"I'm done. It's not worth it anymore," he said.
"Now don't argue with me.
Just get my goddamned gun.
I wanna get this over with."

I found Dan's gun under the sink
with a paper bag of bullets next to it.
"Bring me my gun," he yelled from the living room.
"I can't find it, Dan," I yelled as I dialed 911 on my cell,
my head still under the sink.
"Maybe my wife got rid of it," he said,
"or maybe she moved it.
Check the cupboards."

A few moments later
I walked into the living room.
"I can't find your gun anywhere."
"Bullshit," he muttered.

I sat down in the chair next to his.
He asked me to light a cigar for him.
I lit it and handed it to him.
We waited for the paramedics to arrive.
Dan broke the silence with a story
of a hunting trip.

He was walking in a forest alone.
It was a sweltering day.
He had run out of water.
So he followed a stream down the mountain

where there was a shady wash.
He filled his canteen and drank from it.
As he splashed water on his face and body,
he saw her—
a sleeping deer
curled into a ball.
He shouldered his rifle and aimed.
She jerked awake and struggled to her feet.
He pulled the trigger,
cutting her down.
"I watched that beautiful doe bleed into the dirt."
Dan put his head down.
"That's the only thing I ever regretted," he said.
The ash from his cigar fell to the floor
and exploded into dust.

The Birthday Party

The last time I saw him
was on his ninety-third birthday.
He was in a hospital gown
and diapers.
She was in her diamonds and pearls,
stooped over him,
kissing his face,
leaving a trail of lipstick
on his cheeks and neck.
Her perfume,
which I had told her had gone bad
six months earlier,
wafted through the room.

There were flowers on the table
and birthday cards from his friends and relatives
who never came to visit him.
I wondered if he had told them
not to come,
or if they just didn't want to see him,
or perhaps it was a combination of both.
"Don't live to be ninety-three, kiddo.
The rule of thumb is
if you can't wipe your own ass anymore
then it's time to kick the bucket."

I set down the banana bread
I had baked for him
and some coffee from Starbucks.
"Isn't this lovely?" she said,
her hand on mine.
"You've never just been a helper to us.
You're like family."
I smiled at her.
She took a sip of coffee
and squinted at me.

"Are you my niece?"
she asked a few moments later.
"No, I'm your caregiver."
"Oh, that's right,"
she took another sip of her coffee.
"What did you say your name was?"

As we ate the banana bread
and drank the coffee,
I noticed some travel brochures
scattered on his bed.
"Wake up in a new world,"
one of them said.
"Are you going somewhere?"
"I'm blowin' this joint, honey,"
he laughed.
"By this time tomorrow
I'll be home again,
floating on a raft in my pool.
I'm gonna have a cigar
in this hand
and a scotch on the rocks
in this hand," he chuckled.
"There'll be live jazz,
barbecued ribs,
bare-titted virgins..."

"Hey, I'm gonna go topless, too!"
She kissed his forehead.
He reached for her.
"Birdie, you've been the only one for me
for seventy-one years
and I've loved it all."
I watched him give her hand a little squeeze.
She held on,
her fingers resting
between the I.V.
and his wedding ring.

Distraction

We had to lie to my Mother,
my sister and I,
in order to transition her into assisted living.
She has a touch of dementia
and can't be left alone.
The years of 24/7 home care
have diminished her funds substantially.
The story we told her
is that a water pipe broke in the wall,
flooding her house.
The damage will take months to clean up and repair.
"I just want to go home.
I'm sick of hearing that guy moan all night."
She nodded in the direction of her neighbor.
"I don't belong here with all these creepy old farts."
"I know," I tell her, putting my hand on hers.
"If I don't get to go home soon I'll die.
I know I will."

Trying to distract her,
I pulled some photographs from an old Buffums box.
There were several of my stepfather, Steve,
when he was young.
"Steve used to screw the waitresses
who worked at that coffee shop he always hung out at."
I looked at her,
my mouth falling open.
"Dad screwed waitresses?"
She laughed.
"You're not upset?"
"Well, not anymore. That was years ago.
Besides, I have no right to be."
She picked up a Polaroid, and
studied it with a magnifying glass.
She was dancing with her gardener,

Hector,
his arm around her waist,
her skirt twirling up.
Steve's head didn't make it into the photo,
but I could see his hands lifting
a bare midriff.
A pair of tanned legs in red stilettos
flew in the air.

She threw the photo onto her bed.
I watched her grab the bottle of Merlot
on her nightstand, and
pour it into a crystal goblet
that I brought from her house.
A voice called "Bingo" from the nearby rec room.
Her hand shook as she lifted the glass,
downing the wine in a couple of gulps.
"I'm not one of them," she said,
pointing at an old man in a wheelchair
rolling by her open door.
"Goddammit, can't you see I'm not one of them?"

Dementia

"You look just like my daughter," my mother says to me.
"I am your daughter," I tell her.
"You're not a little girl anymore?" she asks.
"No, not for a long time now."

"I have a secret," she says.
"What is your secret?" I ask her.
She leans in and whispers in my ear,
"I'm younger than you'll ever be."

Doppelganger

I was standing in line at the Home Depot
with a cart full of ceramic pots and soil
when I spotted her.
She couldn't have been more than 18,
a whisper of a girl in red lipstick,
her hair blazing with the same razor cut
I used to wear when I was her age.
I noted the color of her eyes,
the shape of her mouth,
her graceful neck.
There was only the slightest budding of breasts.
The guy in front of me had two shopping carts
loaded with fertilizer and succulents,
which gave me enough time
to locate an old photo of myself online,
looking like her twin.
As I approached the register I turned my phone around
to show her the image.
Her eyes narrowed,
"Why do you have a picture of me in your phone?"
"It's not you. It's me back in 1986."
She grabbed the phone from my hand.
"What the fuck?"
"Uncanny, eh?" I laughed.
She eyeballed me up and down several times
as she rang up the pots,
her gaze falling on my disheveled bun,
my middle-aged hips,
and the muddy paw prints walking across my blouse
and down my jeans.
She asked to see the photo again.
"Are you sure that's you?"
"As sure as I'm standing here."
And as she turned around
to scan the bags of soil in my cart,

I heard her suck her breath in and say,
"Jesus Christ.
 What the hell happened?"

My Hippie Teacher

Hey man, I had a hippie teacher in school.
He had wild curly hair and a beard,
scooped tuna fish straight out of the can with Rye Krisp,
never used mayo,
hated soggy Wonder Bread.

One day my hippie teacher said,
"Everyone write your name on a piece of paper
and pin it to your shirt.
Every time someone puts you down,
every time someone has a laugh at your expense,
every time someone makes you feel less than who you are,
tear off a little piece of your name
and throw it on the ground."
"Why do we have to do this?" someone whined.
"Exactly" is all he said.
By the end of the day the carpet was littered
with our torn names.
And while I was on the floor with my classmates
throwing our mess into the trashcan,
I had an uneasy feeling about my school, my parents,
my friends,
my hippie teacher,
myself,
and the condition of the entire human race.

There was a kid named Steve in our class.
He lied all the time,
even about the small things.
My hippie teacher said,
"Steve, I'm going to give you another chance to tell the truth.
Don't lie to me this time."
All year long my hippie teacher never gave up on Steve,
but Steve kept lying.
Kids were like, "It isn't cool to lie, Steve!"

"Just be real with us, dude."
Steve whipped his head around to face the class,
"Everyone lies.
You're all a bunch of liars!"
Sometimes I think I have a guy named Steve inside of me.
Sometimes I say to myself,
Steve, I'm going to give you another chance to tell the truth.
Just be yourself, man,
and don't lie to me this time.

My hippie teacher
read The Gettysburg Address to us one afternoon.
I liked it so much I memorized it.
Sometimes even now I wonder,
Where is our battlefield?
Where is the consecrated ground?
What is our unfinished work?
What happens if the government of the people,
for the people,
by the people,
perishes from the earth?
How then, shall we hallow our filth?

My hippie teacher appeared in class one day
clean shaven with a short haircut.
We could only stare as he sat at his desk facing us.
Someone started to laugh,
then the whole class broke into laughter.
He motioned for us to quiet down.
Running his hands through his new precision cut
and across his freshly-shaven face, he said,
"I'm smooth on the outside now, kids,
but I'll always be hairy on the inside."

I had a hippie teacher in school, man.
He painted a mural of an upside-down oak tree
on the classroom wall.

It was a long time ago,
but sometimes I still close my eyes
and visualize that upside-down tree
floating in the air.
Its roots are reaching for the sky.
Its leaves are falling in the dirt.
And I am falling
onto this planet,
this battlefield,
this consecrated ground,
where I am still searching for my torn name,
my bucket of lies,
and my smooth,
freshly-shaven heart.

ACKNOWLEDGMENTS

Grateful acknowledgement to the editors of the following publications in which these works or earlier versions of them have appeared:

- Sweaters of the Dead | *Rusty Truck*
- Where did you go, Joyce Finkelstein? | *Rusty Truck*
- What I Know About My Stepfather | *Rusty Truck*
- Spaghetti and Milk | *Ramingo's Porch*
- The Ice Cream Cone | *Trailer Park Quarterly*
- Girl On The Highway | *Nerve Cowboy*
- That Great Big Beautiful Bastard | *Redshift 1*
- The Acrobat | *Chiron Review* | Nominated for a Pushcart Prize by a Pushcart contributing editor
- Girlie Show | *Chiron Review* | Nominated for a Pushcart Prize by a Pushcart contributing editor, received a Special Mention in *Pushcart Prize MMXVI Best of the Small Presses*
- Hollywood Success | *Chiron Review* | Nominated for a Pushcart Prize by a Pushcart contributing editor | *Carnival*
- The Streetwise Barbarian | *V: An Anthology of Poetry*
- The Feral Children of Los Angeles | *Redshift 1*
- Melania | *Redshift 1*
- Dinner at Denny's | *Red Fez* | Nominated for a Pushcart Prize by *Red Fez*
- She talks to me all day long | *Nerve Cowboy*
- Rachel Maddow looks tired tonight | *Trailer Park Quarterly*
- Glorious Morning | *Chiron Review*
- The Sleeping Deer | *Chiron Review* | Nominated for a Pushcart Prize by *Chiron Review*
- The Birthday Party | *V: An Anthology of Poetry*
- Distraction | *Missing Persons: reflections on dementia* from Beatlick Press
- Dementia | Chiron Review | *Missing Persons: reflections on dementia* from Beatlick Press
- Doppelganger | *Trailer Park Quarterly*
- My Hippie Teacher | *Chiron Review*

Girlie Show, Hollywood Success, and Dinner at Denny's were previously published in *Hollywood Church: Short Stories and Poems* by Wendy Rainey | Vainglory Press.

Wendy Rainey's first book, *Hollywood Church: Short Stories and Poems*, was published by Vainglory Press. She is a contributing poetry editor on *Chiron Review*. Her poetry and short stories have been featured in *Nerve Cowboy*, *Trailer Park Quarterly*, *Red Fez*, *Hobo Camp Review*, and *Chiron Review*, among others. She studied poetry with Jack Grapes in Los Angeles and creative writing with Gerald Locklin at California State University, Long Beach.

www.ingramcontent.com/pod-product-compliance
Lightning Source LLC
Chambersburg PA
CBHW071734020426
42331CB00008B/2027